This Poet's Soul

Carter L. Clark

www.ivyhousebooks.com

PUBLISHED BY IVY HOUSE PUBLISHING GROUP
5122 Bur Oak Circle, Raleigh, NC 27612
United States of America
919-782-0281
www.ivyhousebooks.com

ISBN13: 978-1-57197-487-7
Library of Congress Control Number: 2007908557

© 2008 Carter L. Clark
All rights reserved, which includes the right to reproduce this book or portions thereof in any form whatsoever except as provided by the U.S. Copyright Law.

Printed in the United States of America

CONTENTS

This Poet's Soul 1
And Then There is Me 5
It Is What It Is 7
There 9
All The Way Through 13
Don't Hate 15
That's Not My Name 17
Me And Thee!. 19
My Oak Tree 23
Name It 25
Oh, How It All Speaks to My Soul 27
I Love My Black Folks 29
I'm Sorry! It's A Selfish Thing!. 35
Just How I Feel. 37
You Feeling Me?. 43
An Ode to a Walking Stick 45
I Can't Take It. 47
Put Sugar in the Kool-Aid or Don't Touch It At All 49
What in Hell? 51
To Whom It May Concern 53
It's My World 57
Get Me Out of Here! 59
Who Am I Kidding? 61
What Do You Think? 63
Letter to Damian 65
Aunt Gladys Cooked for Us 67
Faith. 71
The Boy Who Believed. 73
The Private Dancer. 79
The Heavens. 81
The Days 83
Unification 85
It's You 87

I'm Looking At Him........................... 89
6th Grade Adult 93
He Fights and He Loses 95
He Knows His Outcome........................ 97
Leave Him Alone 101
Let Somebody Love You 103
Will Be Nowhere Where John Will Be! 105
The Life of Candy Bars....................... 107
Poor William................................ 109
The Dream.................................. 111
There's a Cigarette in My Hand.................. 113

This Poet's Soul
Thursday, February 08, 2007

This poet's soul is vast, deep, and wide
It spans from a grin to every time I've cried
From the morning alarm to a midnight wave
From a continuous laugh to a sexual crave
To a quiet walk to a noisy run
From times of boredom to play dates of fun
From a lonely time to friends all around
From having nothing in common to having common ground
To being broke and not having a dime
From being accused of an uncommitted crime
From racism from whites and others alike
From being hurt by daddy after being given a bike
To churches causing pain and GOD bringing relief
From the pretty green grass to the ever changing leaf
From encouraging words and to words of pain
To being attacked innocently and driven insane
From being tickled to being a shame
From being popular to loosing fame
To having the best and everyone knowing my name
To having plenty of family and having no one to claim
To preaching to the choir and no one hears
From crying to GOD at night for protection from my fears
I can't describe it, all that I've been through
But it's what this poet has experienced—who knew?

This Poet's Soul

From silent nights to when harsh winds blow
From the broken star to its radiant glow
To one phase from another
Not having a sister—only a brother
With friends that are there to having to walk alone
From being accused to having to cast the first stone
From working all night and praying all day
Having to speak up to having nothing to say
From having peace, please be still
From being tired and having my fill.
From standing tall and having to crawl
To having support and having no one to catch me when I fall
From being lied on with me telling the truth
To being opinionated from the start of my youth
From being thought of and forgotten all at the same time
To having to sing with no rhythm or rhyme
From having to hear "it'll be okay"
To often seeing someone standing in my way
From dealing with anger to staying calm
From being tranquil to being an alarm
From being hired and being let go
To being the star and have someone steal the show
From being played like a fiddle or maybe a drum
To killing flowers and having a green thumb.
From giving advice and for no one to listen
To having a hard time loosing weight as the sweat glistens
To eating meat and giving it up
To making sure there's no alcohol in my cup
From playing the piano and writing lyrics to a song
To knowing that everything is right to knowing when every thing's wrong.
From the crazy country to the dirty, dirty south
To speaking my mind and watching my mouth
From sleeping good and staying awake

To having to be real, so real, to having to be fake
Figuring it all out as I go
Sometimes moving fast and sometimes moving slow.
To seeing children cry from what they can't control
But I understand because of my poet's soul
From everyone wanting to be there for them
Watching adults tear them from limb to limb
From being a Callands, Petty, Hailey, and Glass
To being a Clark to living with class.
Struggling against the powers that seem to be
To sitting under my own apple tree
From driveways to byways to the underpass
To keeping up with the time that seems to go so fast
From marriages that surround me to moving and to succeed
To guarding my heart just in case it'll bleed
To all that is and that is to come
What is easy for others and is hard for some
So much more for me to go through
For this poet's soul to experience—who knew?

And Then There Is Me . . .
September 10, 1998

If I could, I would be, a river for all to taste and see,
I'd run so quiet, cool to the touch, knowing nothing, knowing much.
But out of all of the things there is to be
A river would best describe me!

Much like a river I stay on the go
Conquering new things, sometimes fast, sometimes slow.
Much like a river, I'm good at what I do
Dedicated to commitment, to my fellow man I'm true.

Just like a river I sing a song no one else can sing,
I string the instruments no one else can string.
Also like a river, I'm God's created child,
Strong at my strongest point and when I'm weak,
I'm still strong, but yet I am mild.

This river was first created in Java's land
Pushing my way through Norfolk's sand
But out of all the things there is to be
A river would best describe me!

It Is What It Is
April 6, 2007

I took it and turned it side ways
Shook it, cut it, set it ablaze
Rocked it, tickled it, and stared at it for days
Planted it, pruned it, shaped it, used it in a phrase

Then I walked it and fed it
Drove it a little ways down the road
Sold it, bought it again
Placed buttons on it as I sewed.

Next I re-crafted it and jumped on it
I held it up to the sun
I painted it, traced it
All while having some fun.

I slept on it, I drunk it
I gave it to several friends
I typed it, I mailed it
Sold it as a fashion trend.

I wore it, I called it,
Stretched it with a smile
Noticed it on the television
Heard it on the radio for miles.

This Poet's Soul

I carved it, I blew on it
Watered it and dried it with a rag
Hid it, found it again
And stuck it in a bag.

Read it in a book on every page;
I decided to place it in a pot;
Baked it with a baked potato
Dropped it like it was hot.

I bounced it up against the wall
Threw it high up in the sky
Put it in a picture frame
Baked it into a pie.

I ordered it; I canceled it;
I even sat it in a chair
Waved it around; put a bow on it
Sprayed it in the air.

Directed it; governed it;
Used it as a treat
I ripped it; iced it
Covered it with a sheet.

Rolled it, smoked it,
I tried to add a little fizz
Finally, I just gave up and accepted it
It is what it is!

There

It's the wind in the air that takes me there
The cool gentle breeze that flows through my hair.
It's the birds, the sweet melody that they sing
The life of the sun and the warmth it always brings
It's the squirrel's quick movement and turtle's slow crawl
How the summer dissipates just in time for the fall.
It's the cherry and the blossoms on the tree
The apples and pears, and the busy honey bee
It's the fresh cut grass and the dogwood tree
The bright yellow forsythia bush and the deep blue sea.
It's the white clouds in the sky and flat green plain
It's the old black crow and the whooping crane
The tree frogs that join in a chorus at night
The earthworms that work hard to stay out of sight
The brown stray dog that always comes around.
It's the extremely loud cricket and his very distinct sound
It's the black snake standing and the quiet mouse moving fast
It's Vacation Bible School you feel is a blast
The homemade nature trail in its strategic place
The homemade basketball goal and the porch we used as first base
The rhododendrons, hydrangeas, red hot pokers, and variegated hostas too
It's the water hose connected to the house and mom warning you.
It's the smell of wood burning and the gatherings at night
The praying mantis lurking through as mosquitoes put up a fight
It's the big back yard and fast moving cars

This Poet's Soul

Walking or riding to the nearest country store to purchase candy bars.
The honeysuckles with sweet nectar along the road
It's the woodpecker communicating using Morse code
The white picket fence and the garden in the back
The tractor plowing with potatoes in the sack.
It's the tobacco growing and corn stalks high
The sunflowers tall enough to touch the clear sky
Red light . . . yellow light . . . green light . . . Stop!
Mother May I, . . . Duck, Duck Goose . . .
I'm the robber, cousin is the Indian and brother is the cop
Squirrel in the hallow, and My Little Playmate
It's playing house and being a third wheel on a date
It's riding my bike down dirt roads that seem so long
It's all about the country . . . nothing you can do is wrong
The dirt cakes, the mud pies, and my cousin's playhouse
It's sitting beside Grandma on the front seat at church—quiet as a church mouse.
It's Momma singing and the Spirit is high
It's "I'm Almost There" and watching the "Holy Ghost" cause people to cry
It's needing a Pepsi-Cola and a Mountain Dew
The honey buns, Jessie Jones bologna and hot dogs making its debut
Salisbury steaks and mashed potatoes with red Kool-Aid
Walking over to next door to get a fresh new fade
Pork chops, meat loaf, chicken that was good
It's knowing everyone's name in the neighborhood.
Here comes Auntie and fun is about to begin
It's Grandma's cooking that drew friends and close kin
It's playing volleyball in the field across the road
It's being careful of the myth of the wart-giving toad.
Staying with Grandma in the pitch of dark
Occasionally hearing howling and the neighbor's dog bark
The cool of the basement on the hottest day

It's never wanting a friend to go—wanting them to stay.
It's playing church on a Sunday afternoon
It's sitting on the porch and gazing at the moon
It's the sound of music as next door is having fun
It's the music playing and by 2:00 a.m., the party is done.
The thunderstorms that would shake the earth
The season of spring that gives abundant birth
The quiet mornings and coffee perking and Mom is getting ready to go
We're off to Danville, Lynchburg, Chatham, South Boston, or wherever the wind blows
It's the remembrance of Chitterling Struts and bake sales that kept the community alive
The remembrance of waking up in the morning all broken out in hives.
It's the wind that takes me there and there's more that can be said
It's the will I have to keep the memories alive and to revitalize those that are dead
But I'll always be reminded by a simple break in time
Whether it be nature, something familiar, or an evoking of a memory of picking up a dime.
It always seems to take me there; I won't fight it—it's soothing to me
The memories of my past life of how things used to be!
It's the wind in the air that takes me there
The cool gentle breeze that flows through my hair
It's the birds, the sweet melody that they sing
The life of the sun and the warmth it always brings!

All the Way Through
July 31, 1997

Maybe if I sing my song
I'll sing it all the way through.
Without having any interruptions
Or distractions—all the way through!
I hope I can keep me a straight face
As this song goes on through
It caresses notes of pain and sorrow
All the way through!

Maybe if I recite a prayer
I'll pray all the way through.
Without having any interruptions
Or distractions—all the way through!
I hope I can keep me a straight face
As this prayer goes on through
It asks for peace and survival from tears,
and to make it until the very end
All the way through!

Maybe if I moan me a moan
I'll moan all the way through.
Without having any interruptions
Or distractions—all the way through!
I hope I can keep me a straight face
As this moan goes on through

This Poet's Soul

It's a moan for joy and freedom
All the way through!

Maybe if I cry my cry
I'll cry all the way through.
Without having any interruptions
Or distractions—all the way through!
I hope I can keep me a straight face
As this cry goes on through
I cry the tears of unhappiness
Meanwhile, life is trying to beat me too!
I think that I can get through this
—All the way through!

Don't Hate
Friday, March 23, 2007

I woke up in a gold encrusted bed and kissed my wife, Queen Nefertiti, you all know Nefertiti, don't you?
I kissed my children that gathered around the mountain as they began to cry out my name. I responded and blessed them with words.
I sat at the feet of the Son and cried to the Father as He gave me a brand new day.
I stuck it in my satchel and began to set worlds at war. I held on to my day because my controversy causes too much chaos. I'll need it soon when God gets tired of me!
I combed the grass with my breath and blew off steam as I warmed the sun.
I conversed with the seas and convinced them to give me a few more borders.
I only do what I have permission to do but I steal opportunities to show initiative. I think that pleases God.
On my way I smiled at natural colors as the butterflies fluttered to create God's smile.
I pulled out my bowl and mixed a few things and baked a loaf of faith.
I carried it to Nehemiah to taste before serving it to the King.
I finished the meal, hung up my apron, and vexed a choir to sing. The birds sounded so beautiful.
I melted the ice to cool the seas—I needed something to drink. My throat was parched and burning a little bit.

This Poet's Soul

I walked to Niagara Falls with a bar of soap and took a shower that angered the commoners.
They wondered why I couldn't use Fern Spring like everyone else. I told them, it couldn't hold me.
I had to take a nap and rest my head on Mt. Augustus while my feet were propped comfortably on Uluru.
I borrowed a couple of clouds to cover me—I'll give them back when Christ returns. He's coming back soon.
After waking up I defended peace and several nations hated me!
They called me names and tried to make me relinquish my power as they secretly conspired against me.
It's ok. I know how they are. I let my wrath shake their world. As it shook, it registered 7.9 on the Richter scale. I guess I showed them.
I caught a deer as it ran through my living room. I patted it and let it go. I wanted to give it time to rest. It had been running for a while.
I laced my mountains upon my feet and walked through lands. I was careful not to step on my people.
I made it home. My wife had cooked dinner. My job had been done for the day. I gave her a diamond that gave dimension to light and kissed her goodnight. She lay beside me and caressed my shoulders and we held the night and gave birth to morning.

Don't hate!

That's Not My Name
April 6, 2007

I can't keep answering to you, getting the promotion over me, and I'm more qualified.
I can't keep answering to you, making more money than me, and I have the seniority.
I can't keep answering to you, overlooking me, because you have "brighter options."
I can't keep answering to you, knowing all that there is to know about me, because of your research from the 2007 Uncle Tom.
I can't keep answering to you, cheating me, because you know there's nothing I can do about it.
I can't keep answering to getting hurt because of your lies.
You call me a nigger by the way you don't rely on what I say. It's terrible!
I've watched you ask me questions and check behind me by asking someone of your race.
Why did you ask me?
I watch you compliment me with flattering words and tell me how much you appreciate me for the things that I do.
When I do deeds that are notable, I mean extraordinary, you ignore me and praise the one that is of your ethnic group that you feel should be exhorted. That's a mess.
You don't allow me to have an opinion—if I do, I'm the troublemaker
So why not just call me a nigger and get it over with?

I can't keep answering to you dropping my money on the ground because you get self- satisfaction from seeing me pick it up.
I can't keep answering to you pulling out in front of me because it is imperative for you to be in front.
I can't keep answering to you, giving me the "middle finger," because I showed compassion to someone else and it held you up a couple of seconds.
I can't keep answering to the short comments and responses that you make that shows that you are only doing what is absolute necessary for me. "At least I responded."
You make me your slave without giving a command.
How often do I have to be a team player to be the workaholic of the team?
It gets tiring running around profusely to get things done and when the boss comes around, you're the one who got it done. How fair is that?
You make mistakes and light fires and if I don't fix it, then I'm the one to blame.
You watch my steps, you watch my every move, and you listen to my words to recycle them as your own. Plagiarisms!
So, why not just put the chains 'round my neck and my feet and my hands?
It's obvious, we are not animals!
Stop calling me a dog and a monkey!
I speak the same language that you speak.
I am just as articulate!
I can't keep answering to not being equal!
I can't! I simply can't!
Because . . . it's not my name!

Me and Thee!
November 28, 1995

My life comes and goes like the gala lights on the decorated tree
My decisions are made for me, and they are not clearly for me to see
My role is being played similar to the radio and the famous actor on TV
But the only thing that no one can stop is the relationship between me and Thee.

My world is being ran like a track star going for the goal
Not by me, I own nothing that I can control
But the only thing that no one can stop
Is my prayer from me to Thee.

My songs are being song by songsters like Aretha Franklin, Whitney Houston, and Patti Labelle
My words are being told before I have anything to tell
My feelings are being hurt before I think of what to be
But the only thing that no one can stop is my moan from me to Thee.

My words are being written before my thoughts have even come
Not by me, once again, not by all, but by some
But the only thing that no one can stop
Is my song to Thee from me.

My actions are being based upon if I pass or fail
I'm waiting for my actions to be graded; I'm "waiting to exhale"

This Poet's Soul

I'm crawling from the world so high on absolute bended knee
But the only thing that no one can stop
Is my shout from me to Thee.

I am being stereotyped by my magnificent head of braids
The "white" world will never change because I'm suppose to know
all the unfair tricks and trades
But the only thing that no one can stop
Is my communion between me and Thee.

My poems are being written by Angelou and Poe
The world has no time for me, there are not many places to go
The wars of life always come, and believe me, they flee
But the only thing that no one can stop is my hand clap from me to
Thee.

My judgments are based upon whether you say yea or nay
I make very little choices in life; whatever happens I obey
But the only thing that no one can stop
Is my consecrated fast between me and Thee.

My steps are being taken a bit too early for me to think about
My mail is being delivered without me knowing my route
But yet I stay calm, as calm as the sky blue sea
But the only thing that no one can stop is me devoting my life from
me to Thee.

My funeral is being preached before I even decide to die
I'm being buried in the cemetery and not knowing the reason why
But the only thing that no one can stop
Is my tongue between me and Thee.

Carter L. Clark

My wedding is being planned by the world without my knowing
The world never sees me for what I am, no matter how hard I'm showing
I take the hurt, harm, and even the pain up to a certain degree
But the only thing that no one can stop
Is my hallelujah from me to Thee.

My emotions are being played like a Baby Grand piano
Lord, help me stand on my feet and help me to go
But the only thing that no one can stop
Is my seat between me and Thee.

Now I'm running my own life with only the help of the Lord my GOD
With my close relationship,
My daily prayers,
My secret moans,
My songs of praise,
My shouts to GOD,
My sweet communion,
My thunderous handclaps,
My consecrated fasts,
My unknown tongue,
My glory hallelujah,
My seat in heaven,
And my devoting my whole entire life,

Just me and Thee!

My Oak Tree
(Another poem written from my adolescence)

My oak tree, so strong and tall
My oak tree has leaves and all
My oak tree symbolizes my faith
Strong and stern it symbolizes my faith

My oak tree cannot be knocked down
My oak tree keeps me working towards my crown
My oak tree symbolizes my faith
Strong and stern it symbolizes my faith

My oak tree can only grow
My oak tree ages as years go
So far it's only seventeen
Strong and stern it symbolizes my faith

My oak tree is planted in GOD
Even when the wind blows hard
My oak tree got its nutrients from church and home
My oak tree grows, romps, and roams

My oak tree feels the sun
As it moves through its bark until it's done
My oak tree is a Baptist Christian tree
I believe in it and it believes in me.

Name It

Name the name that will set me free
Name the heart that will let me be
Name the wall I can't go through
Name the task I can do
Name the beer that won't get me drunk
Name the song that has no funk
Name the river I can cross
Name the tooth I can floss
Name the tear that I can't cry
Name the death I can't die
Name the feeling I can't feel
Name the card that I can't deal
Name the grass that I can't cut
Name the nut that ain't a nut
Name the sound that I can't hear
Name the horror that I don't fear
Name the word that I can spell
Name the place—Heaven or Hell
Name the shoe that I can't wear
Name the trouble that I can't bare
Name the dish that I can't clean
Name a cliché that I mean
Name a glove that will fit
Name the sweater that I can't knit
Name the pen that I can't use
Name the one that I can't abuse
Name the car that I can't crank

This Poet's Soul

Name the ship that I have sank
Name the grade that I can fail
Name the pathway that I can't trail
Name the person I've named unknown
Name a wind that has not blown
Name a tree that I can't cut down
Name the face that just won't frown
Name the spirit I can't kill
Name the spirit that I can feel
Name the name that will set me free
Name the heart that will let me be.

Oh, How It All Speaks to My Soul

Oh, how it all speaks to my soul
And entices the ball to start its roll
I can't believe it's finally true
How things have changed—my perception—my view
Who can change it or rearrange it so
Don't think about trying to stop its flow
Just sit back and relax, wait and see
As what is spoken brings victory
Watch me, see me, and let it be
GOD spoke it and it is setting me free

I Love My Black Folks
February 11, 2007

I love black folks
There's something about their flair
Did you know they can walk in a room, never say a word
And you will still know they are there

Yes, I love my black folks
And especially the excellent things they do
They're in a class that's not in school
And they only compare notes with people of the same hue

Look at how they wake up in the morning
And thank their GOD for another day
Notice how they kiss their spouses and say hi baby
They hug their children and send them on their way

It's very unique how black folks wash up
And begin to dress with an awesomely unique style
I like the way they check themselves in the mirror
And validate themselves with a smile

How we are able to take the pain
And transfer it into the very best musical sound
That makes other races travel for miles
Just to be around

This Poet's Soul

Oh how I see so much beauty in blacks
Their inventions, their glory tracks

The spirit that they have
Really makes you move
The anointing that you feel
Gets you in the groove

The way they speak
The words they use
The silent movement
Non-verbal cues

But look at the way they get up
And go to work on time
Yes sir, no ma'am, look at how they work
Hardest in their prime

Look at how after they have provided for the day
The check, they'll see it later on
They head back home to be with their family
Until time for friends and fun

Notice how they build friendships
One hinges on another
Women's friends are all sisters
And men's friends are all brothers

They build the bonds that are so tight
No problems can leak through
Let something unfair begin to take place
And they'll stand right beside you

Carter L. Clark

Yes, I love my black folks
Until the very end
The trailblazers, the showstoppers,
The setters of many trends

They match their shoes with everything
Hey, that's their classy style
Make sure they have some blingidge on
We've been sporting that for a while

No we haven't overcome
But am working hard to succeed
Trying to make sure our race is pure
No matter the shade—they're filled with blackness since the day we were freed

We love church and family reunions
And gathering under the same name
The spades, dominoes, hallelujah, the joy, the laughter,
We're so comical, having too much joy to place blame

They act, sing, model, cook, write
They build, invest, create, and take flight

They walk the walk and talk the talk
And always show the personal side
They teach, preach, role-model, and are lovers
They take challenges in stride

I love my black folks
They can be whatever they want to be
Their roots are deep
And are as strong as an oak tree

This Poet's Soul

I love my black folks, I love my black folks
They keep me with a grin
I see so much of how we've grown
As I look back from now to back then

Don't you just love black folks?
Never boxed in and how they keep their pride
They are always "doing their thing"
Their blackness is just that wide

From being chained, dragged, and killed
To being hung on a tree
They've got something to be proud of
The slaves' blood flows through them
They've got the victory

They can walk on water, turn water into wine
And even cross the Red Sea
We can climb the highest mountain, handle the lowest valley
And always find GOD on our knee

I love my black folks
I love their flair
I love their facial features
And their hair
I love their arms
Chest and breasts
Their hands, legs and thighs
And all the rest

I love their personalities
And their attitudes
I love their wonderful dispositions
Even when they're rude

Carter L. Clark

I love my black folks, yes indeed
The chocolate, caramel glow
Their smell is of the pride of Africa
Through us is the honor of our Motherland that we will always show

One of the reasons I love black folks
Is because it's where I belong
I fit in; because I'm black
We all sing the same song

I love my black people; they are who I am
And I want everyone to know
I love my black folks; their strength carries me through
Black folks, don't ever change—oh how I love you so!

I love my black folks!

I'm Sorry! It's a Selfish Thing!

It's a selfish thing
I am so ashamed to say this
But it's a selfish thing
I missed the meat of everything that has happened
Because—it's a selfish thing
My focus was on me
My life, my hopes, my dreams, me—all about me!
Maybe it's guilt speaking
I told you, it was a selfish thing
I was aware
But in spirit, I wasn't there
In spirit, I missed Katrina
I now feel their pain
Though their pain is impossible to feel
Unless you were there
I missed the whole thing
I told you—it's a selfish thing
I missed my time to cry
For those who had to die
I was too busy concentrating on me
Why? Because—it's a selfish thing
I'm not alone
I'm just the only one that will admit it
But there are others that can admit the same thing
Why? Because—it's a selfish thing
They won't do it because it's all too inhumane
I'm just a brother trying not to go insane

This Poet's Soul

I'm sorry!
I'm sorry!
I'm sorry it happened!
I now ache inside
I know I'm days late
It was too late when I cried
It's a selfish thing
And I'm sorry!

Just How I Feel
Tuesday, March 20, 2007, 11:00 P.M.

For some strange reason I feel as if I could die tomorrow. I really work hard to push this thought aside.
I sit and wonder very hard how to get off this tumultuous ride!
I guess it's from trying to live down the actions that I made today.
It could be guilt or Satan's plot to try to lead me astray.
I'm searching hard and questioning my heart and trying hard to understand.
This is ridiculous, to me it's so ridiculous, to conquer this problem at hand.
Should I worry, should I cry, should I tell my loved ones goodbye?
Should I grin, continue with my spin; continue to look for ways to fly?
Should I write a letter of sorrow and pain to explain my mournful farewell?
Should I just keep pressing higher and higher and ignore the story my spirit is trying to tell?
Maybe it's my candor, my need to confront, or my powerful way of exposing other people's lie.
Maybe it's how I look at people and cause convictions and eyes to cry.
I'm not powerful (I have no power of my own); I have no control of anyone. I can't cause anything to be.
But what I feel inside, I just can't hide, this feeling keeps worrying me!
I can't escape! It's probably just a farce—a game being run on my poor soul.

Should I be worried? Take it as a warning from God? Or should I view it as Satan trying to take control?
God, I pray, lead me in the way of all that I've ever known to be good.
Help me to survive and live day-to-day and see the other side to this "spiritual-hood."
I feel great pain. I see the pain. But, what it is, I do not know!
I want to cry. I can't cry. Maybe there's a sign beginning to show.
If God wasn't in control of what is concerning me then I wouldn't be able to be so stable.
So, if I'm not mistaken, Satan is trying to plant fear and make me disbelieve that God is able.
I must be getting ready to go to another level. I must be heading to the next stage.
Satan is evoking a lot of different feelings. He keeps applying pressure. It's an uncomfortable rage.
I guess that tomorrow I'll wake up and I'll head to work and not be scared that something will go wrong.
I'll get up, get dressed, go on my way, and prepare my day as usual singing my theme song.
"I'm Looking for a Miracle" pumps my heart and gets me expecting good things at all times.
I know that there will be some kind of opposition—but I'll go looking for the best of times.
I won't let my actions of today get to me. I won't let them persuade me that I've screwed up bad.
Because I have to expect the unexpected I'll prepare myself—work to be glad.
I wonder if this is a small part of how Jesus felt when knowing that He would die?
Something made Him pray extremely hard for us and for Himself as he sweated blood and began to cry.
The difference is that He didn't have to wonder if Satan was playing a hand in how He felt.

He knew the truth—He is the truth! No one can truly know exactly how He felt!
But I know how I feel. This feeling is real! It's mind-boggling and is challenging me inside!
I sit and wonder very hard how to get off this tumultuous ride!
Tomorrow, it'll all be over and tomorrow, I'll let you know how it all ends.
I'll tell you whether or not I'm desecrated by enemies or if the day allows me to make new friends.
God I pray that all will be well and I'll work towards helping Your will be done.
I've gotten off the course that You have plotted for me all for the sake of decadent fun.
No more! No more! No more will I let this be. I can't keep feeling this confusion in my inward heart.
Shhhhhhhhhhhhh. Listen to the beat of my heart!
Tomorrow will be fine. I know it will. I won't worry! I'll get my rest! I'll talk to you tomorrow—I'll tell you the rest. I'll live tomorrow to tell you the rest!

Wednesday, March 21, 2007

At work today the boiler, that was remotely stationed, malfunctioned causing an electrical fire. The lights flickered, rooms were filled with smoke and familiar smoke scents, and the floors shook. The fire alarm didn't sound. We evacuated the building after seeing other fellow occupants from other departments walking steadfastly out of the building while waving, signaling for everyone to get out of the building. We could have died! Because God had me in the right place at the right time I was able to warn others to get out of the way of the strong possibility of danger. I really do think that it was supposed to have been a tragic day of demise. But that day, people experienced God's great mercy like never before, and still false gods were given unmerited recognition.

Thank you Jesus! You spared our lives one more time. One day we'll notice, listen, and learn for the sake of kingdom building and so that we will ascertain what we need to do in order to do our part in helping Your will to come to be done! To God be the glory!

Just how I feel!

You Feeling Me?

Sometimes I feel
    Like my time has/is flown by
    But yet I live
    It's not my time to die

Sometimes I feel
    Like my hope is gone
    JESUS is right there
    But I feel alone

Sometimes I feel
    Like everyone has forgotten me
    Everybody's looking at me
    Yet, it's not me that they see

Sometimes I feel
    Like I'm in a world so cold
    Plenty of possibilities
    I have no one to hold

Sometimes I feel
    Like I have a twin
    Who's sitting right beside me
    Then, it's back to being just me again

Sometimes I feel
    That I'm almost out of sort

It gets hard to think things through
But my plans seldom come up short

Sometimes I feel
    Like I'm a waste of time
    As if I've committed some crime
    Like I'm being punished without reason or rhyme

Sometimes I feel
    As if I am so defeated
    Acknowledged as cheated
    Leaves me feeling heated

Sometimes I feel
Yes, I do feel!
Picking up on everything that's fake and real
Leaving me in my corner tight and still
Dealing with devastating issues that seem surreal
That constant pace that breaks my will
I guess I'm stuck in these feelings until
I can finally find a way to sit back and chill

But don't ever think that I don't feel!

Because I do!
What I feel, is what I feel!

An Ode to a Walking Stick
(Another poem written from my early childhood)
January 15, 1997

I used my walking stick everyday
To beat the evil away
To walk down the road, the long cold road,
Through the muck and miry clay

I seek no one, just having fun
As I walk along this road
Just me and my walking stick
That's why I sing this ode

My walking stick is my best friend
That will be here until the end
If anyone messes with my walking stick
I'll be there to defend it; swift, like the wind

My walking stick so sleek and tall
Saves me from the harm
From the snake, the toad, even the dog,
And the tree that scratched my arm

I'm still a travl'n down this road
Just this walking stick and me
With it by my side, and GOD as my guide,
Heaven is my destiny.

I Can't Take It
March 26, 2007

I get weak inside
I lose my pride
I sit and cry
Because of my tears
They lead me to fears
Because what I see
Is really bothering me.

I encourage a world
Full of doubt and despair
A faithless world
That has forgotten that GOD is always there
A world so hurt
They reject the very sight of care
It's because of what they see
And it really bothers me.

They shoot down hopes
Possibilities and dreams
They desire no suggestions
At least it seems
Their aspirations are low
They're moving slow
Walking by sight
This guides them away from the light

This Poet's Soul

They claim they're free
But they're not and it's bothering me.

On the side of their beds
Alone in their car
Shopping alone
Waiting by the telephone
Up all night
No family to hold
Their heart gets cold
Lost in doubt
Can't figure things out
These things are what I see
And it really does bother me.

Therefore, activate your faith
Get up and do something
Last I heard, something was better than nothing
Renew your mind
Let GOD take control
Forget about what's not
Focus on what can be with all your might from the depths of your soul
Don't be afraid
Go ahead, try, and make it happen
Progression is your boat and GOD is your captain
Make it to the top
And as you're doing it—let me see
Because all of this doing nothing
Is really, truly, bothering me.

Put Sugar in the Kool-Aid or Don't Touch It At All

My Kool-Aid is red and sweet
It astounds everyone that I meet
I ask them, will you take a drink
Of my Kool-Aid that is red and sweet?

Don't dip your finger in if you're not ready to commit
Because my Kool-Aid is da shizznit
It'll keep your mind, body, and soul fit
It'll keep your fire burning and your candle lit.

Don't sip, go ahead and gulp me down
It's the best Kool-Aid in the whole town
My Kool-Aid will turn your frown to a smile
It'll make you walk a mile and then wait a while
I keep some made because that's my style
My Kool-Aid flows like the river Nile
To drink it all, don't be greedy, yo, that's foul.

What in Hell?
Sunday, March 4, 2007
All of a sudden so much matters
Life, careers, sexuality, everything
Where is this coming from?
This feeling—this feeling of needing and wanting
This feeling of pain and anger
This feeling of fear
Where in hell is this coming from?
All of this stuff mattering
What's going on?
The pain of the present
The anger from the past
The fear of the future
I was doing well
I had my mind focused on God
My hand in His hand
What happened?
How all of a sudden everything matters!
Why won't these feelings leave me alone?
How is it that they are being fed and are being made stronger and stronger?
Why is all this stuff mattering?

To Whom It May Concern
March 11, 2006

I hate the things I think about
I hate the things I fear
I hate the things that try to control me
The things that stop things from being clear.

I hate the way you look at me
I hate the clever smile
I hate the way you walk in your shoes
And the way you judge mine as I walk a mile.

I hate the way you critique me
And say that I'm ok
I hate the way you look at me
As if you wished I'd stay out of your way.

I hate the way you sing your song
I hate the way you try to sing mine
I hate the way you smell my food,
Thump my melon, and taste my wine.

I hate the way you dress me
You dictate what to wear
I hate the way you hold me
And tell others you don't care.

This Poet's Soul

I hate the way you touch me
And rub across my skin
I hate the way you read me
From without—within

I hate the way you tell me that
You'll always be there
I hate the way you leave me
In a lethargic stare.

I hate the way you move me
And shout and scream my name
I hate the way I'm left holding the bag
Filled with the guilt and shame.

I hate the way you take me
Into a wonderful world unknown
I hate the way you sweet talk me
On the telephone.

So now I stand free in chains
And the world will never know
I hate the seeds you've sewn in me
And how the seeds will grow

I'll see the sun, a brand new day begun
Eventually, one day, everything will change
I will welcome all of my opportunities
And will find nothing, any more, strange.

I'll like me, I'll love me
And all you've helped create
I'll smile again, I'll finally win
And then I'll be straight

Carter L. Clark

So go ahead and laugh at me
With all your haughty pride
I'll overcome you, yes I will,
With victory as my guide

I'll go on in Jesus' name
And make it 'til the end
I'll steer clear of your wicked tactics
And all the tricks you send.

No more acts of frustration
And telling my self lies
No more thinking less of me
No more midnight cries

No more saying words that hurt
Speaking of weight and size
No more using my resources against me
All for my demise.

There will be no more scaring me
And placing fear in my heart
I'm starting the race all over again.
Surprise! It's a brand new start.

Turn around! Stop looking at me
And go on to someone new!
I'm writing you to let you know
That you and I are through!

So bye, bye! I won't miss you!
And I don't wish you well!
You tried your best to destroy me

This Poet's Soul

Which means, you tried hard to fail.

Don't you dare mourn for me!
I will be just fine
I'll make it through (I made it through you)
I'll definitely get what's mine.

So now I can begin to grow
The trash is bagged and gone
The lightening has flashed, thunder rolled
And the wind has finally blown

Watch me as I go to new levels
And be more than I thought
Conquer land I've never seen
And watch troubles come to naught

Sing a song of joy everlasting
Sing a song of praise
Sing a song that rings with cheer
Sing a song of happy days!

Hallelujah, thank you, Jesus
All is finally well!
Praise GOD, Glory Hallelujah
Because all . . . is . . . well!

It's My World
Saturday, February 10, 2007

I imagined owning the world
Bringing a smile to some little boy and girl
Being a dad and holding an orphan's hand
Helping the elderly to walk and stand
Providing money to pay everyone's bills
Giving, sharing, being empathetic to the way everyone feels
To make every child feel loved and fine
Seek to end war to bring peace of mind
To plow everyone's gardens and produce crops for miles
Feed every homeless person; just to see their smiles.
I would love to provide homes for all in need
Everyone will go to college and 100% will succeed
People will laugh, and dreams come true
Every hand will have a glove and every foot in a shoe
Insurance: affordable and Bentleys, too
Everyone having the same: each château having an excellent view
Everyone will have money, only dollars, no nickels, pennies, or dimes
Full of casual conversation and definitely no crimes.
Taxes, no more, we pull together as we get everything done
We'll build; we'll work all while having fun
Those who entertain will do what they do best
While the workers who've worked will sit back and rest
Music will be different, something for everyone to enjoy
Nothing nasty, only the cleanest is what I will employ.
Flowers will be pretty, bright, and everywhere
No sickness or dying due to the finest health care

This Poet's Soul

We will do all that is necessary to take care of Mother Earth
We will honor her resources as she continuously gives birth
We will follow GOD'S rules and keep HIS order
No nursing homes needed. We'll be the perfect son or daughter.
We will value time and make use of our days
Democratically vote our yeas and neighs.
If I make one step, I'll help you make two
The air will be fresh because everything will be new.
The future—no problem! The past—gone at last!
The present—perfect! Opportunities—vast!
Life—precious! Continuing one day at a time
Lies—be gone! Faith—abound! Truth—sublime!
Heavens—open! Earth— free! Hell—shut down!
Republic—strictly for the people; Bliss in every town!
It's my world and you're welcome to come
Welcome . . . to my world!

Get Me Out of Here!
Sunday, March 4, 2007

How do I get restored?
Back to the way I used to be
Believe in what I used to believe
Look for things I used to see

How do I get back there?
Place the things back in my hands
Handle my problems like a pro
Stop paying attention to others' and make my own demands

How do I start over again?
Step out on faith and act on what I know
Though the wheels stop turning
Make the prosperity flow

How do I get it back again?
That ability to be who I am
How do I reclaim my awesome ability to roar like a lion?
And, yet, be as gentle as a lamb

How do I start it all over again?
Step out of old shoes and into new
Believe in myself and what I believe in
Go back to what brought me through

This Poet's Soul

How do I get out of this bed that I've made?
The bed that now allows my feet to hang
That has cataclysmically thrown me into a state
Wow, how it has stopped me from doing my own "thang"

How do I get out?
Why am I trapped here?
Why are all the doors closed?
Somebody! Anybody! Get me up out of here!

Who Am I Kidding?
April 6, 2007

Who am I kidding
Life ain't never been good
It's been one problem right after the next
People lying, cheating, stealing
Leaving me with the feeling of always having to fight internally while they sit back and feel good.
It looks like my day just won't come
I've missed my cloud that had the silver lining
I've just had a hard time
Enough is enough already.

I'm on fire inside
I felt my heart literally hurt as a sharp piercing pain walked through it
It's from all the stress
All the dealings of people who refuse to do what's right for their own selfish sake
Their personal gain is the only thing that is important
The power struggles between mere mortals to get nowhere is ridiculous
The use of words that prove nothing because there is no couth in their everyday living
But, yet, they feel a step higher than I.
Why
Because of the hue of my skin
Their cockiness within
Their disregard of the consequences of sin

Their obsessive needs to win
They needing the security of a better end
Why do I have to suffer because of their egocentric ambitions?

My altruism is gone

What Do You Think?
October 14, 1995

Do I walk the walk that tells many lies?
Or, do I talk the talk that there lies my tries?

Do I sing the song that says I'm the best?
Or, do I crawl the crawl that cheats the test?

Do I sit in the seat that says I'm dignified?
Or, do I lie the lay that my sincerity will notify?

Do the words that I speak defy your character or meaning?
Or, does my attitude decrease your state of being?

Do the thoughts I think explain your ignorance in truth?
Or, do my eyes see the sight that cuts similar like a shark's sharp fine tooth?

Do I cry the tears of being inconsiderate?
Or, do I carry the genes of my grandfather's trait?
But my question to you, what do you think?

Letter to Damian
Saturday, June 3, 2006

What's up?
How are things going?
I am sure that I am probably the last person on earth that you thought you would hear from.
I wanted to write you for 2 reasons.
The 1st reason is because I wanted to do something to let you know that **it's all good!**
Mistakes are meant to be made and we all make them.
Of course they sometimes lead us to a place where we don't want to be,
But we experience mistakes in our lives for a reason.
But do me a favor,
Make sure that you learn the right lessons from this mistake.
Nobody knows what you are going through but GOD.
I'm not going to even try to pretend that I know what you're going through!
Please, make sure that you find someone that you can trust that has some common sense,
And talk to them about the situations that you face everyday.
Somebody is willing to listen.
GOD has put too many people on earth for us to have to go through mistakes alone.
So please don't keep it bottled up inside—it will only make you explode again.
I learned as I became a man that part of being a man is to know how to manage (control) your emotions

Without anybody getting hurt.
I don't say this about everybody,
Damian, but you are much too good of a person to be sitting in negative places because of mistakes. You're smarter than that!

The 2nd reason why I am writing you is to say thank you.
Sounds weird, huh?
Well, you helped me to realize some of what JESUS CHRIST went through when HE was beaten before HE was hung on the cross for our sins (that's why GOD forgives us when we ask HIM for forgiveness).
At that moment, when everything went down (repeatedly hit me for a reason unknown),
I kind of understood a little more about how JESUS CHRIST might of felt.
That experience helped me to grow spiritually stronger. So, thank you!
Well, I've made you read enough now,
Keep your head up and know that I am here if you need me!
I'm praying for you!
Remember, GOD loves you and so do I.
Be Blessed!

Aunt Gladys Cooked for Us
(In Memory of Gladys Rebecca Glass Callands, 1921–1997)

Pass the butter for my biscuit please
I would like some of that macaroni and cheese
Oh look, there's the bowl with the green peas and black eye peas
And broccoli that knocks you to your knees
Shake some salt; too much pepper makes you sneeze
Here's some honey straight from the honeybees.

Wow! That looks good. A honey glazed ham
Along with my buttered biscuit, I could sure use some of that homemade jam
I better hurry up and grab it; I only see one candied yam
Guess what's coming out the oven—a rack of lamb.

There's sausage, and chitterlings, and even fish
Get the wishbone from the turkey and make a wish
The baked and the fried chicken is my favorite dish
The meatloaf and hamburger steak is delish.

The ribs are done just past me a few
Put turnip greens on the plate and while you're at it add a couple of deviled eggs, too
The cornbread is good, the crackling cornbread is better, and I love the beef stew
Aunt Gladys, can't nobody cook this food like you!

This Poet's Soul

The homemade pizza is ready to eat
The pig ears are done and so are the pig feet
Now, I thought the neck bones couldn't be beat
Until I tasted the potato salad, that was really a treat

The chocolate cake and sweet potato pie
The Watergate salad was awesome, and that's no lie
The Jello mold tastes so good I could cry
Ever wondered why I'm fat—the chocolate mousse is why.

Mashed potatoes and gravy—mmmmmm divine
I ate all the watermelon. Aunt Gladys said that was fine.
To get the boiled corn and string beans you have to wait in line
Strawberry shortcake is coming up next. We have to unbutton our pants—that's a sign

All the food that's out here, we can't even name
And Aunt Gladys is still cooking just the same
You know cooking is one of the ways she got her fame
She makes a rice pudding that puts everybody else's to shame.

The pork chops are done and is hot as can be
I asked Aunt Gladys to make an egg custard just for me
I'm eating coconut pie that was my plea
I'm tasting everything mentioned from A to Z

Spaghetti in meat sauce is ready, don't delay
I'll bring out the macaroni salad on a silver tray
I love the way Aunt Gladys seasons certain foods with Old Bay
And these fried apples taste way better than okay

The baked beans are great and the pintos I ate were good from the start
They say Aunt Gladys' stewed tomatoes are good for your heart

Carter L. Clark

I want to take food home but I'll need a cart
Pack me some lemonade it was good and sweet—not tart!

Look at all these people enjoying Aunt Gladys' meal
To miss one day of eating at her house would be unreal
The way her home cooking makes you feel
Everyday I'll meet you at Aunt Gladys' and that's a deal.

Aunt Gladys cooked and never made a fuss
One thing you could always count on—Aunt Gladys cooked for us!

Faith
February 26, 1994

Sit back, relax, and forget about all your troubles.
Let God take care of them; let Him float them away like bubbles.
Feel no hatred, badness, or sadness;
Let God take care of your heart and fill it with great gladness!
Trust with all your heart and don't you ever doubt!
Just remember, let God have it! He'll bring you out!
When you feel you can't take it!
Lift your head up! Better days ahead with God you can make it!
I don't think I'll ever stop talking about what He has done for me.
He calms my fears and He helps me to see.
Even when you feel like you've been hit with a ton of bricks,
With God on your side you will be able to take a lot more licks.
Whether it's your cousin, uncle, aunt, or even your closest friend tearing you down.
No matter what they say, always wear a smile and never wear a frown.
I am leaning and depending on God!
Why shouldn't I? Moses did when he looked to God and stretched out his rod!

Faith!

The Boy Who Believed
January 12, 1997

    If there was a poem so sweet, not hard to follow by,
    Is the Holy Bible, written by those who still prophesy
    Matthew, Mark, Luke and John all followed by God's rule
They were all once changed by God when they once lived a life so cruel.
But now we have all once been just like them, who once was not unchanged.
    It is up to us to believe, and magnify God's Holy Name.

One day it was cold and snowy.
Jack Frost was nipping at everyone's nose.
A little boy walked in his home to greet his mother,
With his cheeks the color of a rose.

Boy: Hello mother, how are you today?
Mother: Fine, little one, I'm glad to say.
Boy: Well, are you all already for tonight, as we watch the stars above?
Mother: Oh, little one, it's too cold tonight! Let's stay in the house in our love!
Boy: Well, maybe, I can go to Billy's and play with his toy train?
Mother: No, little one, you must stay here and wait for your father and brother, Cain.
Boy: Why do I have to wait for them, they've never waited for me!
Mother: Oh, hush dear child! I won't hear of that! They'll have gifts, just wait and see.

This Poet's Soul

After waiting a full hour
Father and Cain came waltzing in.
The boy was so excited
He ran from the front of the house to the end.

Cain: Hi mother, how are you? We've made it back from town!
Father: We are so glad to see you two, we only brought one gift. (The little boy frowned.) Everything was expensive, and many pennies were passed.
Mother: I hope you didn't go over our budget dear. If you did the money won't last!
Father: That is why I serve a God that is honest and is true. Seem like to me, ye of little faith; you don't know what to do! Now, Cain, look in my satchel and grab that little box.
This is for the little one.
Boy: Oh, no! Not again? Socks!
Cain: You don't know what's in it. So be quiet and open up.
Boy: Well, it's a book! Another one to sit over there by the giant ceramic cup.
Father: No, it's not just a book to sit over to the side. It's the Holy Bible; the human's ultimate guide.
Boy: What do I need with a Bible to tell me what to do?
Father: I should have whooped you more when you were younger. Come here! Let me explain it to you!

After the father explained to the boy
What the Bible was used for
The little boy was interested, he began reading
His mind began to explore!

Boy: "In the beginning God created the Heavens and the earth."
(The little boy began to read.
The first chapter of Genesis was exciting to read
He read it with intense speed.)

Carter L. Clark

Well, that's enough of this chapter tonight,
But in the morning, I'll be reading Revelations with fright.

As the little boy slept,
He dreamed a vision,
It was about trust in God
And forgetting about his past beliefs in superstition

He saw an angel, Oh how beautiful
It was awesomely caressed in white
He thought "How Heavenly!" as he laid there
And watched it slowly walk out of sight.

The next morning the little boy woke up
And got dressed to go to school
He read a passage out of the Bible
Unknowingly he read the "Golden Rule."

He got on the bus
Teaching the word
He told how God's eye
Was on "some bird"

He told about God's Son
"Who died for you and me."
He told how he made the deaf man hear
And how he made the blind man to see

After a week had well passed by
News had hit him that he would surely die.
Die of sores all over his skin;
Blistering open, trials were about to begin

He was also told that his father was dead
As he laid in the hospital in his death bed
He never said "Lord why me?"
But he kneeled in prayer, on bended knee

He continued to read the Word of God
As Satan attacked him, which he felt was odd.
He personally called the reverend that he knew
And asked a numerous set of questions
That randomly popped out of the blue

Preacher: There will be times when you are strong
You'll have trials that will come along
Trials so great you won't know what to do
Trust in God, he'll see you through

The little boy thanked the preacher
And kept a sweet simple smile
He said, "I can do it! I will pull through
These hard but simple trials."

Weeks passed and even months
The boy never ceased to pray
He knew that God would hear his cry
And surely make away!

His mother came and brother too
They both came in and asked him, "How the heck are you?"
With the same smile he replied,
"Please don't curse, come stand by my side."
The mother said painfully and began to cry

Mother: Baby, give in! Curse your God and die!

The little boy laughed to hear such a sentence
He kept praying and praying and said

Boy: You need to get on your knees for repentance
Mother: I'm only trying to help you to feel better and moving once more
Boy: To give my soul to the devil who is rotten to the core?
I refuse to lie here in my affliction,
I'm sorry, out of my room! I'm giving the benediction.

Cain: Listen to momma you stubborn fool
Boy: Leave and God bless (he replied without loosing his cool)

The boy continued to pray without ceasing
He kept reading his Bible not stopping for any reason
His family had left him; his only hope—which was his father—was dead,
He kept praying and finally Satan fled

He began to get better
The pains fled
He shouted all the way out the door
From his bed
He spoke in other tongues
And had joy within
He screamed I have been purged
And redeemed!
He went to his house and said
Jesus is the glorious
And looked at his mother and brother
And said, "Through God I am victorious"

Thank you God!

The Private Dancer
December 3, 1994

There's a Private Dancer inside of you
Even though you get confused He still knows what to do

No matter what goes on or what may happen
Inside, the Private Dancer is still a'tappin'

Even inside expect Him to show you the way
He helps and calms your feelings; He will always stay!

Whether you're singing, shouting, stealing, writing,
Playing, rebelling, crying, or fighting;

The Private Dancer will always be there
To make everything alright and to make sure that you care

To care about everything including other people's feelings and their situation
I know some people would say He enters in like an inundation

Even though you want to go off, in other words, tell someone exactly how you feel
When nothing happens, you can really say that the Private Dancer is real.

Another name you could call this Private Dancer—you could consider this word—He's Peace

He makes you feel happy and causes all bad things you feel inside to cease

Could God be this Private Dancer inside of all of us?
Yes! It's the Holy Spirit who's the one that puts a halt to all the fuss!

The Private Dancer is not the author of anything that deals with confusion
Never ever say that the Private Dancer is just an allusion

The Private Dancer's work is never left undone
Believe it! The Private Dancer is the essence of God, the Father and His Son!

The Heavens
January 27, 1997

I looked into the 1st Heaven and saw the bright sunshine. I wanted to travel further just to find peace of mind.

I looked into the 2nd Heaven and saw the big bright moon. Then I knew I was almost there to arrive to be with God soon.

Finally, I gazed into the sky and said the 3rd Heaven, there, I will be. God said "all in time, my child, my face you shall see."

The Days
April 27, 1995

Though the days have passed
And are gone on their way
Passing through other zones
Leading on a brand new day

Maybe today won't be as bad
As yesterday was
Making it through insults
Usually, I wonder, who does?

While this day moves on
Let me contemplate
I need some time to think
The day is gone, keeps moving at a steady gait.

Though the days passed
Gone on about
There's no time for stopping,
Certainly no time to doubt!

Well, the night is here
And is about gone just the same
Where is the time going?
Who is really to blame?

This Poet's Soul

The days bring tiredness, weirdness, among other things
Or is it really the days?
Maybe it's the people
And their distinct and passionate ways

It could be the people really altogether
Pushing away all those days
No matter what, they still keep going,
No day ever stops and stays!

Unification
Thursday, February 8, 2007

I called the wind the other day
He really had a lot to say
He spoke of how things often change
He spoke of how unnecessarily things are strange
He changed the temperature as he made me feel odd
He spoke so much truth all I could do was nod.

I ran across fire this afternoon
He told me that things would be purified soon
He shared of how things had gotten out of hand
He spoke of how righteousness was on demand
He said he's waiting for the day
Where he can flame up and get carried away.

I visited water at his place
He spoke of how things are a disgrace
He told of how he once fixed it all
When he flooded the world at the MASTER'S call
He said to me "it's a sad day ahead"
And those without righteousness will be eternally dead.

I heard from earth and we talked awhile
He was tired of all that he'd seen that was vile
He felt as if he was falling apart
And he reminisced of how he had such a strong start

He shed tears of moisture and made fertile the ground
And its inhabitants made a mournful sound.

And we cried out loud, GOD how long
As we all gathered together to sing our song
We looked towards heaven to await the LORD
HE smiled as HE finally saw us all on one accord
The FATHER gently said to the SON, "it's time"
And CHRIST returned.

It's You
Thursday, February 8, 2007

Touch my back and feel my soul
Give me warmth and remove my cold
Lift me up to a higher place
And place a grin upon my face

Let me flow in your deep wide vast river of care
Your warm breath breathing lets me know you are there
Grab my hand and place it right
Whisper my name the rest of the night
Now tell me what you think of me
As you wrap your leg around my knee
Caress my shoulder and move up my neck
Nibble on my ear with much respect

Move to my cheek and around to my lip
Into my mouth let your gentle tongue slip
Once again hold me, hold me, and hold me tight
Be sure to tell me that things are all right

Scream my name and say it loud
Say my name as if you are proud
Say you feel me and can ease every pain
Your crazy love drives me insane

Oh the thought of your body next to mine
Soft gentle fingers going up my spine

This Poet's Soul

Yes, that's the spot—so divine
I'm glad that your love is mine all mine

Keep me; love me, in order to survive
Without a doubt you, keep me alive
There's none like you and it will never change
Having you with me—that's not strange

I love you; I need you, and will always be there
I surround myself with you—you are my air
Don't ever leave me—don't ever go
There's something that I want you to know

You are my love and peace of mind
You are my joy and one of a kind
I can't be distracted by any one else's spin
A love like this, it's a sin!

I'm Looking At Him
April 2, 2007

I'm looking at the perfect man
I see him standing with a medium height in stature
His legs are short but are capable of carrying him anywhere

His feet are a size 14 and are considerable in width
I see the hair is stubbly short with insurmountable hints of curls and waves
His broad shoulders are capable of carrying anything

His hands are hefty and are needed to hold bulky things
His chest stands out proudly because he knows his worth
I can see this man's eyes are fixed into a steady gaze.

His senses are strong and never lead him astray
He uses them to protect his family and lead them the right way
He's beautiful because he is skillfully crafted as a design by GOD

His muscles are defined, noticed, and strong and his heart pumps steadily
His lungs take in deep air to keep this well-tuned machine oxygenated
I can see that his cheekbones are high, and are the highlight of his face

This Poet's Soul

I notice his nose occupies every perimeter of its space
His lips are of high dimensions and are the salmon that puts pink to shame
His hindquarter has been strengthened because of his tribal dance

The veins in his hands remind you of a freeway as they travel up his arm and into his neck
His facial hair is raw and demands attention as it gives credence to his jaws, lips, and chin
His wrists bares the marks that is evidence that he had once been chained

The life lines in his hands resemble the stripes that his SAVIOR bore for his sins
Though his speech is not fitting it grabs the attention of his listeners; everyone listens to what he says
His fingernails carry dirt of hard laborious work that is not in vain

I'm looking at a man with the teeth that tears meat from its bones; he has a throat of laughter, and is capable of a thunderous tone
From inside comes the nectar that is needed to provoke birth to nations
So much potential; so powerful

He is a black man
His bones are filled with rhythm
His strong candor is something no other man can deny
He's serious about his business and can handle his own

I'm looking at him taking control with nothing but his unadorned presence
His quiet demeanor teaches him everything that he needs to know
He's a man and is to be respected as one

Carter L. Clark

I'm looking at him
I can see him
The view is something to see!

Very few, for some reason, can admit his contributions to the world
Where would the world be without him?
He is the pattern for others to carbon copy

He intimidates the haughty
He gives pride to the modest and deprived
His compassion deserves a just reward

Many are jealous just by looking at him
But I see him
He makes me proud

He carries himself with masculine elegance
He's got it going on
I see him
And he makes me proud!

6th Grade Adult

Why do I suffer like I'm locked up inside?
I've lost my stride; I've tried and tried!
And now, and now, it's my turn to give up
The restlessness inside of me; the gunk that's about to erupt
The underachievement; no victory
The spirit of slumber won't seem to leave me
And now, right now, I feel as if I'm in jail
I saw myself kill a man
Using nothing but my bare hand
But then I stopped my imagination and began to understand
And now, even now, I feel like I'm in Hell
I race against time to get THERE fast; where? There! And I'm getting there first!
Jumping over, crawling under, the generational curse
Overcoming victory with defeat
Practicing deceit
I have failed to guard my spirit inside,
Such a sweet, sweet, noble spirit I hide
Working not to lose touch with a Holy Spirit inside
I need someone in whom I can confide
And now, right now, even now, I don't know what to do
I'm trapped inside without a clue!
My mind is sleepy but my body is awake
My mouth only yarns for my spirit's sake
It's hot and dry and dark in here
There's hatred, disgust, despair, and fear
There's vile and lewdness, and stubborn dreams

Torment, and persecution and demons grouped in teams
There's so much for me to handle as a 6th grade boy
But I have no time to pick up and play with my favorite toy
I have an extreme amount to get done
I'm also the adult with errands to run
And now, even now, very, so much so, now
I am inundated with steam
I sit in my stubborn position
And now, right now, I realize
What's no surprise
From all my cries
That it's true
I'm different from you
Because I'm in between the two
Who?
Me, not you
Accept it Ma, Pa it's true
You raised me so I could have a childhood like you
Yes, you did it and there's one more thing, too
I'm a 6th Grade Adult
With only the adult thing to do!

He Fights and He Loses

He can't understand why things are the way they are
He fights and he loses.
Awakens to another day and can't understand why things are the way they are
He fights and he loses.
The part of life given to him—he's not allowed to control
He sleeps in hope to wake up, but to wake up in a world that he can control
He fights and he loses.
He's tired of the grownup world forcing him to be a child
He's tired of the bold grown men making him meeker than what he wants to be and making him extremely mild
He's tired of his family giving demands
He's tired of trying to make everybody understand
"There's nothing any can do" is his mantra for life
He can't understand why things are the way they are
He fights and he loses
Awakens to another day and can't understand why things are the way they are
He fights and he loses.

He Knows His Outcome
Wednesday, April 25, 2007

He knows his outcome
As he stands there looking out of the window
He knows his outcome
He looks out of the window thinking about what to do next
But it doesn't matter, He knows his outcome
To escape a world that constantly leaves him behind
He looks for ways in his restless mind
"How do I get out of here?" rings constantly in his mind all the time
He stairs at his arm, scratches his head
Gazes out of the window
Switches the weight onto the right leg
He sighs with pain, anger—searching for relief
Contemplating something, wondering, battling with his belief
He can't sit down. Can't find comfort in a chair
Declares himself all alone with 2 people sitting there
It's not the end. He could care less if he dies
All of his tries always lead him to the tears that he cries
All because it's obvious to him
He knows his outcome
I'm facing him—staring him right in the face
"Death is the only option."
Death is the only option?
"You can't possibly mean that," I toil inside
Thank GOD that deep inside he really refuses to believe that
Thank GOD he won't accept that

The room is quiet; should I make noises to throw off his train of thought
I've talked to him
He's determined
He knows his outcome!
One sleeve up and one sleeve down
Arms are folded standing in a planted stance
His back is to me—he faces the wall
I feel safe because I'm wrapped in GOD; I believe he is in the room protecting me
I feel the HOLY SPIRIT constantly releasing me of fear
HE knows the condition of this young man's heart
The young man would rather choose to handle things his way
He knows his outcome
I told him that "this storm will pass,
If he hangs in there the storm won't last."
If he embraces the present and accepts the future
He'll make it through and be okay
The past has him locked up; won't let him go
The past is moving fast and the now is moving slow
He's been hurt inside; it's made him mean
He craves for danger; to try to commit what he's already seen
GOD, help me to get him to understand
Life is better alive and not as a dead man
But he props himself against the window pane
Stares at the wind as he listens to Satan cry out his name
He continued to sigh as it appears that he's trying to ignore
As he turns slowly and begins to walk out of my classroom door
He says, "It don't matter, I don't care anymore"
My compassionate heart took a plunge as it grounded the floor
"Forget education, I've seen all I want to see
I'm sixteen now." His words shook me!
I walked down the hall and tears ran down my face
To see a hurt young man

Carter L. Clark

Is such a disgrace
He knows where he's been
Where he's going
And where he's from
He never stopped walking
Because this young man,
He knows his outcome!

Leave Him Alone
Friday, March 23, 2007

How many more insults can you give a child?
How many more ways can you change a smile?
How many more ways can you make him fill insolent?
How many more ways can you keep him trapped in your tent?
How dare you sit and make him do all that you want him to do,
As if you're perfect and he's not doing what he's suppose to.
If he wants to color with the color red don't make him change because you want blue,
And if he asks you why he should change, don't get offensive.
Explain it just like you would want someone to explain things to you!
If he speaks different and sometimes can't comprehend,
Help him to make it in society. Teach him how to blend in.
So what if he can't read on the level that you would like,
What if he is having difficulty with multiplication and math problems alike?
And what of it if he can't be quiet and enjoys rapping the hottest rap songs?
Give them an award for being able to discern and settle unfairness and work to right all the wrongs!
You've given them a life of gangs and chaos. You've taught them to be the way that they are.
How far does the apple fall from the tree? Anyone? Anyone? Let me answer. Not far!
So, let him go out at night and you never say anything edge wise,
When he steals the car, hit someone, and meets his own demise.

Don't be mad; don't be sad, because he is only doing what he has been raised to do.
You concentrated so much on yourself that your nightmare has come true.
All you did was hit and beat and never explained why.
He never heard "I'm doing this because I love you,"
"This hurts me more than it hurts you," and "Doing this makes me cry."
How can you expect him to wake up one day and be a better man? He's doing what you have taught him to do! Leave him alone! He's doing the best he can!
Why give looks of disappointment and words of ridicule and shame?
It's because of you—all because of you—this young man is not to blame.
Instead of buying shoes, and brand name shirts maybe he ought to have been bought a book,
Let's master making this child cultured from the heart and not just with a certain look.
Give, give, give, give, and give and afterwards give some more. The right things—what he needs,
Be there to be a Band-Aid just in case his delicate heart bleeds.
Don't let the thug talk fool you—he is smarter than what he leads you to think,
Just because he says "pingwen" instead of penguin don't turn your nose up because you suspect that he will sink.
Don't prejudge—he's seen that enough already.
What he needs is stability and respect and love that is steady.
This goes out to all races—take heed and be sure to keep him in the zone.
Encourage, support, exhort, and RESPECT—But most of all, leave the child alone!

Let Somebody Love You

Just let somebody love you
Let somebody wrap their arms around you
Surround you with kisses
Hold you in their arms
Let them let you know that everything is okay
Just let somebody love you

Stop fighting
Stop looking for a way out
Just let somebody love you!

Let them take the pain
Let their heart beat for your heart
Let someone else care for you
Let them take your pain
Just let somebody love you!

Answer when they call
Let them catch you when you fall
Let them be your all and all
Let go of the past; tear down your wall
Let them be true to you
Let them do what they desire to do
To help you simply make it through
Just let them love you
Let somebody love you

This Poet's Soul

Give into the care
Allow them to be there
Just let somebody love you!

Stop pushing everyone away
Stop and listen to what they have to say
Stop handling things by your self day after day
Just let somebody love you!

Let them be your confidant
Let them help you to a brand new start
Let them help you bring things to an end
Let someone be your friend
There's no need for all this pain
Don't let things and people drive you insane
Somebody is got to help you through this rain
Don't live this life living it in vain
Come on, be serious about this thing
Let someone help you change the song you sing
Just let somebody love you!
Let them love you!
Let them love you!
Let them love you!
Just let somebody love you!

Will Be Nowhere Where John Will Be!

Come along little John
We have a long ways to go!
We have hills to climb,
Bridges to cross!
And people we need to know!

Come along little John
Please don't be scared.
I know you've really had it hard
And are tired, but there's a lot of road
To cover that has been prepared

Come along little John
Come on. Don't be slow.
You've been beaten very hard
And your feelings have been hurt.
God has declared that there is no more punishment for you to undergo

Come along little John
You were born an angel of truth
Can't believe you made it this far.
Not far to go. Keep pressing on
And soon, very soon, regain your youth.

Well, you've finally made it Little John
Now I've got to go back

Through the winding dangerous path,
And through the muck and mire
Nothing, anymore you lack

Little John is now safe with God
With no more problems to see
Those who persecuted him for no reason
Will be nowhere where John will be!

Happy! Happy! Happy! Happy!
Happy! John has the victory!
Those who persecuted him for no reason
Will be nowhere where John will be!

The Life of Candy Bars
(Another poem written from my early childhood)

One day *Baby Ruth* was sitting on her knee.
Then came along *Mary Jane* and they both climbed the tree.
Mr. Goodbar made them get down from out of the tree.
Then *Mr. Goodbar* made a *snicker* as he sat down to listen to his favorite *symphony*.

Now, Mr. *Hershey* had *butterfingers* as he made his *tootsie roll*.
He received a *kiss* from *Mary Jane* and then he caught a cold.

Mr. *Reeses* was happy because it was *payday*.
He strolled down *5th Avenue* with *zero* in is way.
He walked in the office and asked for his check and received *100 grand*.
They gave him half of Mr. *Worther's original* check and he did an impressive head stand.

Mrs. *Almond Joy* walked in the room crying.
They thought she was *nutrageous* but she said her cats were dying.
Her poor cats, *M & M*, were just too old to live.
They put a *mound* of dirt on their grave until the grave wouldn't give.

Back to *Baby Ruth*, she played with a bug.
She stepped on it, made it *crunch* and swept it under the rug.

That's the life of candy bars. Who will write the rest?
Because remembering other candy and candy bars will truly put your mind to the test.

Poor William

"Mrs. McCoy, how did I fell disheer test?"
"Well, William, did you do your best?"
"I did what I could, and what I knowed to do!"
"Well, you failed the test, what am I suppose to do?"
"Cut some slack! Curve deeze grades!"
"Well, I'm only giving you what you have made!"
"Give less work! This is only elemetry school!"
"Well, you would make better grades if you would follow directions and rules! Poor William. You'll do better next time!"

The Dream

Sit down! Shut up! Get it together!
I'm the substitute so let's gather!
Sit in your assigned seats! Get out your pencil and paper! There's going to be a test!
You better be prepared and you better do your best!

If you make an "A" it's still an "F"!
After doing that, we still have more work left!
Joe, shut up! Kim, sit down!
Everybody smile! I better not see a frown!

There's no library, and definitely no P.E.!
You have already made an "F," Ray! If you have a question, ask me!

I ate the principal, and I'll sit on you!
I'm the substitute! I'll do what I want to do!
Jeff, get the broom! Saundra, get the mop!
It's time for manual labor, hop to it! Don't stop!

It's the beginning of the day, close the door!
Ebony, help Saundra! She missed a spot on the floor!

O.k. let's stop! It's time for lunch!
You all don't need any, you're a stubborn bunch!
I have brussel sprouts in my book bag!
Get them out! Eat them raw! Tony, go outside and wash the school's flag!

This Poet's Soul

My board is dirty! Derrick, I told you to do that!
And while you are at it, sweep that mat!
Who are you? Looking in my classroom?
You're a teacher; your life is completely doomed!

Kids grab her! Stuff her in my closet for later!
I'm going to swallow her whole like an alligator!

"No! No!" Timmy woke up in class!
"What is wrong?" asked Mrs. Glass.
"I dreamed about our substitute! I'm glad she's not you!
The substitute in my dream, if she was here, she would try to eat you!"

"Well, everything is o.k. Get to work!" said Mrs. Glass.
Everything became peaceful in little Timmy's class.

There's a Cigarette in My Hand
(Another poem written from my early childhood)

This poem is dedicated to all the mothers in the world who have had to make it through life in a single parent home with only GOD and a cigarette in their hand.

HEY! Look at you and look at me
And tell me if you'll stand
Well, I'll tell you one thing, I will,
I got a cigarette in my hand

Bills will come and bills will go
And will you understand,
I done been through it all, and made it
With a cigarette in my hand

One husband came and the other one went
Because they both had the same demand,
I tell you now it don't matter,
I had a cigarette in my hand

A loved one passed and loved ones gone
And I made it, putting it in GOD'S hand,
He woke me up, started me on my way,
And put a cigarette in my hand

One completed; the other one on his way
Done made it through college sand

This Poet's Soul

I laughed and thanked GOD for it
While puffing that cigarette in my hand

Now look at you and look at me
They carrying you to insane land,
Here I am with half a scruple left
And a cigarette in my hand

I've been good, I've been nice,
And obeyed GOD'S command
I believe I'll make it all the way
As long as I got a cigarette in my hand

Now if I die before I awake
And go on to the Promised Land,
Tell everybody that you know
I made it!
With a cigarette in my hand